THE BARBAROUS CENTURY

The Barbarous Century carries the reader into poetic realms that are both brutal and joyous. A book for our times.
— **DOIREANN NÍ GHRÍOFA**

In *The Barbarous Century*, Leah Umansky's voice, intelligent and intuitive, reaches into each poem to investigate the wondrous and terrible condition of humanity.
— **RACHEL ELIZA GRIFFITHS**

When we talk about books of poetry being generous, we're talking about collections like Leah Umansky's *The Barbarous Century*. Here are poems that lay out everything they've got. Poems that call forth a cast of voices ranging from W.B. Yeats to Daenerys Targaryen to Azar Nafisi to Emily Dickinson to Don Draper. Poems that 'spuddle' towards romance, that cherish 'the bristle and the fat,' that invite in 'another delicate storm of possible.' What fullness, what symphony, what verve Umansky has conjured here! *The Barbarous Century* is a wild, magnificent achievement.
— **KAVEH AKBAR**

LEAH UMANSKY **THE BARBAROUS CENTURY**

EYEWEAR PUBLISHING

First published in 2018
by Eyewear Publishing Ltd
Suite 333, 19-21 Crawford Street
Marylebone, London W1H 1PJ
United Kingdom

Cover design and typeset by Edwin Smet
Collage by Leah Umansky
Author photograph by Jen Fitzgerald

Printed in England by TJ International Ltd, Padstow, Cornwall

ISBN 978-1-912477-05-0

*The editor has generally followed American spelling and punctuation
at the author's request.*

WWW.EYEWEARPUBLISHING.COM

for Mom, Dad, and Faith, always

Leah Umansky
lives in New York City and is the author of
Domestic Uncertainties (Blazevox, 2012) and two
chapbooks, *Straight Away the Emptied World*
(Kattywompus Press, 2016) and *Don Dreams and I
Dream* (Kattywompus Press, 2014). She is a graduate
of the MFA in Poetry at Sarah
Lawrence College.

TABLE OF CONTENTS

3 THIS IS A HISTORY OF SWORN WAYS

1
THE LOST JUST
WITHIN REACH

I HEARD THE SPARROWS AGING

I heard the sparrows aging
a devouring call
a broken spring, there, turning

a sputtering of what sounded like keys
the lost just within reach
tenants of the past, nearly a-hold

oh, the horse and the rapture
the horsefly and the rupture

       to a sleepy pungent
       a beautied terror
       a backward giving
       and the rain coughing

let the gutter turn operatic
I will sing of the heart

I DREAMED UP A LESS VULNERABLE NETWORK

with wolves, scales, and endnotes. The wholes acted with me,

in key – I mean the linear tug was the love-line
and the love-engineers cobbled together to salute

me, as one who is 'heralded', 'cleft', and 'ragtag'.
[Note: I am not the arch-villain of this poem. You are.]

You are. You are. You are. *All of you are.*
You bittered, jerk-packeted, dark-usherers.

The whirl of each star is a quiet crusade,
where I wave a red banner, suffer, and hum my tune.

In the crux of each nightfall, my shield fawns
over bloodshed. [This is not a sweater-clad expedition].

I am un-illuminating what glitters. I am un-narrating
this story. It will drop now.

                    She will rollick with the tinkers,

those innovators who mistake an ending for a side way.
Here, is your side way out. Push this, then pull.

And here is your own flagship, but she salutes the night-rowers,
their pitching and pioneering, their penny-jar full of grace.

Their sky is still-dark and wonder-felt.

In love, there is terror, and in terror, there is a-passing,
but in the stone quiet moments, there is a rush of wind.

There, is her banner. She is there in the afterglow. See her.

WHERE ARE THE STARS?

I am a galaxy of one, of one whole, but my whole is centered. It's a ring of pity. A ball of fire. I am not a liar. I know what I feel, and I know that there is so much that I want to be a part of. Outside my center of one, there are others I pine for. Within my pine, lie slices of dusk, coolness and mist.

I am a magnet that pullsandpullsandpullsandpulls. I am pulling you now, but nothing is charged.

The self is mapped in certainties. I am certain that I can measure this in words.

Flaubert says, 'The principal thing in this world is to keep one's soul aloft.'

I am keeping my soul lofty. I am keeping my soul inside my darkest chamber. I have pinholes of sun that star out. I have pinholes of night that deepen and swing. There are constellations shaded with breath. I connect them with my want. I connect them with my wanting and my waxing and my waning and my waiting.

The center of the self is a star.

(aren't all stars dead?)

FOR ALL THE IMPOSTERS THINGED OR KINGED

Small girls dream awhile.
The most are slipped graces,
and many graces are slipped.
Yes, there would come a rope,

a lady who takes heartbreak,
or a lady who saddles ill-luck.

All storms since you have given in.

I have been operating from nothing,
with no thing in hand, but *these*.

As a shelving of moving moss,
I am ever on the lookout
for a gorgeous sentence gone,
any gorgeous thing.

No glancing.

Mine is not one common.

SESTINA

The time is naturally over. It is another morning. Lie
Still, but declare the carpet of marigolds at your tongue, yours. Raise
Your lips to the flock of sunlight at your door and tell yourself to man
Up. There is no mourning now. Another day is another brilliant readied
Start. Another delicate storm of possible. Stand
Straight. Look away from the blinding. It is best

Taken with a whirling steam of night. I can't remember the last time I thought it best
To stand so completely honest with the world, with myself. We lie.
It is so easy to lie, but I know that even lies have colors and they stand
Out against the dark. How can there be a living gem inside me when I cannot raise
Another hope to the sky, another winged account of song and shade and readiness.
I ready my wild, it is a fiery double, but I do it before the skies and the sea, before man.

I said I was falling apart. I said in a stern voice, and with a whopping fear: *Man,*
I am falling apart but it was not so. All was gone in a flowering of what is best.
All was gone, as if a great thinning flattened all of the worst feelings into a ready
Furling, the way joy can be defensive, the way fire can be tinkered into flame. Here's a lie:
I can handle my emotions. It is ruining me. I sing myself the cadence of tongues raised
High in song, in might, in glory. Glory. To come to the whirl of calm, one must stand

15

Aside. One must jump from the fear and see the circling below. Spiral the hurt, stand
Back and rise at the way the sound of your heart blossoms. Manage
The way a bond is unbreakable until a thousand flowers raise
Their heads to you in scent. Send the rising in your throat away and swat it. Best,
What I like best is how the way you need is never destroyed. The way all those who lie
Know the fright within their city. Their body's green, yellow and red.

You can bring yourself to a standstill, if you choose, but red
Almost always means stop, means rest, means stand
Back and breathe. I might cover myself in flight, or sky, or clover, all to lie
Myself into believing that I am stronger than my stresses. I tell myself, *man*
Up. I tell myself, *nature is more than glorious*, and I feed myself the best
Choices, the best meats and berries. Look, raise

A glass. Raise two. Why don't we just raise
The whole damn bottle of red?
Some of us might say what we feel is best.
Some of us might inspire other elements to action, but I stand
Alone and it is not evolutionary. It is barely manageable.
It is practically a lie,

But one worth telling. I am bold in this lie I raise to my lips.
I salute the readiness of myself and I manipulate the rest.
For the joy of no longer standing alone, that bold sprig is best left to blossom.

HARD

It is hard to quiet the blackberrying pain.
The little chronicles, the streaks, and the intimate workings.

I will face this by red-winging my truths.
I will push my blues into orchids.

I'VE INVITED THE REJECTION

★

I've invited the rejection. I let it into the room to fester, to germinate, to diffuse and to ruminate in its art. For it is an art, at the end of the day, that choosing. All that inviting.

I said I invited the rejection. I did. I said, 'Here is a bed for you. Here are clean towels. This is where I keep the body lotion. This is how to turn on the night light. What kind of tea would you like?'

★

The thing is I'm tired. Are you tired? I'm tired of these things that flank me. Stop pushing, pull. This door. That room. This step. This handle. This train. This grip. This transaction. This checklist. This handshake. This smile. This frown. This jealousy. This pining. This pining. This pining. This pining.

★

Are you telepathic? I have a friend who can see spirits. I can't see spirits, but I can see you don't want to talk to me. No one wants to talk. The wound is in the image. It's in the way you imagine the other.

This is a place of flowering. I tulip in the idea of it. I juniper in the sighs. I don't want the imagining, I want the real. See. Can you see? Say that you can. Say it with me, *I see you*.

I've invited the fearful. I reject all of these faces until I am faced with the face that is not fearful, with the face that feels, with the face that knows that no one day is the same. Time is not in

bloom. This is the time where what we love is not what we say or share or feel. Love something. You should love something so intently that it becomes a destination.
'I would invite you in, but...'
But, contracts the breath. I want it extended.

★

Each day is a taught-fear. We are conditioned to make waves. I want my wave to be glorious. I want it to be tipped in the freshest white. I want it to rise moonbound. To swoon in foam.

★

Fullness. I am alone in my fullness. I am alone in my blend. I am alone in my moments, but am seeking more. To be fuller. To be more full. Full of all of the stories and despairs. Full of the horrors we are all capable of. We are also full of horror. The real horror is when you think you are the only one, alone.

★

Do you feel your own wounds? Do I feel my own wounds? Do I? Feel what, wounded?

★

Haven't I laid out all I've got to sell? It's one thing to paste over it; it's another to break the mold. I am breaking it each day. Every path to my door. Each fallen branch. Every pothole. Each lamplight. It is more to say that there is no fear. What is fear but an untuned instrument? Tight are my strings.

THE LOVE-ORPHANS

This is a galactic train of scattered drift. Alone in the flickers. A left galaxy. I haven't found the cosmic: this is a scrofulous mess: light *should* connect to light. We are filled with so much space, so much willing-mash, and so much that is a faint wreck. I want something flung-over. I want some other singular star. Whatever is bright. Whatever is brighter-still.

Cluster around me.

In this city, we are a string of little pegs in the night. I emit light. [nothing] I halo what I love for others. [nothing] I am stumped. [still, nothing] There are other possibilities Yes, there are other solo-slingers, but I want bigger. I want to pull a planet into my swing, maybe a moon. In this harbor, in this void of space, I can go the distance. I will not go dim. If light seeps from my fingers, let it connect to a distant starry-depot or a rocket ship for which only I know the code.

I will construct my own team: the love-orphans. If collisions, combustions, or just mere fuses are the worry of others, I will go rogue.

THIS COULD BE NOSTALGIA

Let us count that you regard
        and I regard

the changing of the tides
and the sea of the last.

            We are tenaciously taking the tides
            in favor-abandoned ways.

We are contempting the contemporary,
        or co-tempting the contemporary
        into a kind of sin.

We are doing more than channeling
        when we laugh
        or when we strategize.

In-my-day, I was a believer.

        in my day   in my day

the dial-up had a certain purr
that ruffled my roost
That's lost now.

            ★

Now, you, you, let alone with the golden.
Let the golden wilt and wild.

We can construct the past.
Potshot the pristine.

Here, coordinate my sprawling.
Together, this could be nostalgia.

HINGE

Hatch the tale.
Hinge the hero.

This will be the device.
No fears will haunt.

you must

the locality
the vision

I'm telling you too many secrets,
but in every light, look.

Under all the tempers,
sparks.

How will I know what it will be like?

a ruin
a think
a crux

more than a response
or this current hour

To what edge can we cling?

This has affected me.
This pause is alive.

What flame?
What skeleton?

Here's the last line:
(like a hum and a hero)

A girl musting,
a girl wanting,
is pierced with desire
and furied.

Something is percolating:

like landing
like storm
like need
like rumor
like plunge
like survival
like seize
like heeling
like heeling
like heeling

wrong
wrong
wrong
wrong

in all of us

a catastrophe of one.

TURNING OVER PHRASES

Listen and listen good, I clicked [add to spell-check] when I saw that your name turned red. I blushed and thought: *How romantic; How very 21ˢᵗ century!* That's the beauty of this felthed time. I can spuddle with what I deem romantic. Tug it, tweek it, and tune it till it's just right. Each digital act is darged by a display of affection or gratitude, attitude or charm.

There is a bit of me, here, between bone and heart-bone. A bit muffled, but still plush. It has been too long; too gone, since I've felt this kench. An interior *kvetching,* here, beneath the breast. I am looking at the digital for something heart-felt, something coded, HEART! Something worth sharing. Something worthy of an investment.

But then again, I am a salesman. (My father's daughter). My words, a financial gesture between myself and my word-bank. I am selling you an aesthetic experience. I touch-type [x][x][x][x] and a word is now forswunk and forswinkled. I am *so* endearing, *so* enduring. Can't you see I'm being genuine? This is potentially profitable. Don't you want to cash-in? The heart is a loaded weapon.

[Did I say weapon; I meant, *investment.*]

THE STRIVING

In the way-worth and the side-spent.
In the way I break,   in the way I lend.
In the way-sought and the way I went,

                              move aside.

In the way of horns and motors, in the way of musings over.
      In the nights and the songs,
in the weekends and groans, I remain low on guesses and turns.

I have fingers lost in the search and the cold-fishings.

In the back way,   in the water way,
in the way of more, I have crept too long in the striving.

What more has been decided?

In the before-ways,   in the after-ways,
in the breakaways,

I will only say, *soon*.
      Soon.

FORGOTTEN CENTURY

There is a door; I am the housekeeper of the history behind
that door. My rich inadequacies are a career of recents: a file
of settings. My dirty linens are a non-linear myth.

What naked flame? I like my blues muscular. I like my breath
to be as wide as a wooden spoon.

This is not a warrior's helmet. This is a scarf, really.
This is how we sense the world.

★

If all of the world's value is forbidden, and wracked, then
what of the saving?

Take these lingering questions; the darkest dark of years; the
hunted manifestations, what of their experience? What will
their equations equal? What will their fates unfold?

I've been careless. Greedy in an age of recurring nightmares
and borne-struggles.

I might not say *barbarian*, but I fight behind screens.

This is the way the world will go:

>one heartbreaking betrayal of what will be over
>what was
>one heartbreaking betrayal of what we
>should've kept.

Nothing is ordinary.
The door of the future could be through this page.

THIS IS AN OLDER GOAL

All of my life, I've wanted to look back on my life. All of my life, I've wanted the already-made-adventure. All of my life, I've wanted to be the thankful woman, the sharp woman, the loved woman, the loving woman, the accomplished woman, the beautiful woman, the well-read woman, the traveled woman, the aged woman, the respected woman, and the cultured woman. All of my life, I've wanted the focus of a hawk, to look back on a life of worth, that accompanied heartbreak, and know the strikes and the spares, to know the flight and arrow of my life, to know the ditches in the terrain, and the curve of time.

★

all of my life starts today

the girl I once was
the woman I wanted to be

these arriving shes
their teetering hearts
the molt of their lusts

I want to tell them,
there will be time for gingering
time to procure and to harvest

back::back::back

sketching of winds
peppering of days
jailing of whens
all the pastured dreams
            rustling
all the populated nothings
            doubting
all the ebbed yearnings
            saturating
those rubied fragments
a-wreck and watching

their eyes are sky-cast, sun-clipped and cold

THIS IS A LOVE POEM

I will herald my ghosts

I will braid our pasts
I will unlid secrets
I will forest bruises
I will strange love
I will cabinet the lies
I will haunch the hurt
I will expunge order
I will temper the liked
I will pale the bad
I will away the soiled
I will hush the undone
I will stab the fault
I will dream the lie
I will sweet the love
I will still the brood
I will play the stars
I will pronounce the naked
I will index chance
I will darling the crookt
I will soldier the dreams
I will pageant the breaks
I will cycle the jitters
I will sing the caring
I will belly the upset
I will feast comfort
I will turn the certain
I will empty the dark
I will flame the barbarous
I will shun the ills
I will repine the not

I will listen

Sound is at the bottom of everything

I will draw out the word from our throats

DOING

1
There is no word for the opposite of feminism I tell a student.

2
Toni Morrison said, in an article in *The Guardian,* that, as citizens, we are always told by the press, *so and so tried,* and she notes that no one *does* any more.

I do. I don't know where I'd head. But I've known yearning, and this off-season needs to end. I will not be what is left over. I will be the dirty work, the hopeless grind and the sweet heaven. I will scrawl these whispers into walls.

Speak to me. I am doing this.

3
I am urging myself to express more frustration. I felt that this was a strange stream spraying. I felt this was nothing to get hysterical over, but still, a situation that needed voice. We always need voice. Nothing is picture-perfect and if that means we bring the pace to a stop, so be it. I am urging myself to be less meticulous, less focused, to take what is given to me, and to take what I need.

Still, do men have such thoughts?
No. Because there is no word for their struggles.

4
I am a bringer. I bring to the table. I bring to my life and to yours. I beg at the true mystery of life and wonder if it is just a little stifled voice. Let me put it another way. We all want to step out into a day and know we are good, that we try our best at all times.

THIS IS A POEM IN WHICH I CANNOT BUT BE

fold me
in the heartpluck
among the elmed
& the sinking
and the short fur

the drop
now drawn

the live light
lit

the once kind
cooled

more
sore
lore

       interested?

     (no)

there is joy here

there will come

a tug
a slip
a sway

always

      a filling

always

            a lull

tender || ender || ought

THIS SPEAKER ISN'T TALKING

Anyhow, that is all that came of it.
Life is about the best   [way::elixir::gift]
It was the very agony of agony and I buttoned it shut.

Dear Neighbors,

Please put down the [phone::gun::flute]   *I've taken it all outdoors*
with the hounds with the girl in me   *with the saltlicks*
with the underpinnings   and the millet   *and the grain*
          and the sweet and the pain.

In any great open [field::heart::sky]   there is an
anecdote   or antidote.

Here, is when I dote on it all.
                                        There, is when it all pings
                                              and pongs.

It is the saddest story, this life.

We have to wander in it for stars, bone over the pennies
curate the lightning in our own trimmings, and gather what
is full-blooded, generous and rare.

FOR REALS

This is what opportunity looks like: a tugging at knots.

It's in the toggling that we get stuck. One foot always straddling,
and sometimes we toil.

      We weave. We unweave. We leave without looking back;
      we leave without   straightening.

It matters to me. Not the mattering itself. Not what is matted,
but also the unmattering itself.
Things, matter! I want to do. I want to make and I want the
making to do wondrous things.

I want the wondering to rise around me. I want it to surface on
the upper lip.

[I never cared for crusts.]

      If you want me to really go in on it, show me
      what I'd be risking.

So you know what opportunity looks like::come closer.

Opportunity knocks. I want to answer. [I do]. So you know, of
course, I want to answer, but certainly, I'm cautious. I see the life
I was meant to have. I see it knocking. It's not at my door yet,

but *Yes, Sir,* when my bell rings, the bell will break. I
will repeat this mantra: *Don't deny yourself.*

Denial is tough to swallow, but the delight is peachy. I
want digestion

and the satisfaction that follows.

•

FORCE

1

At night, the stones are heavy in my hand.
At night, the stones are heavy in my mind.
At night, the stones are heavy in my heart.
I want to be someone. I want to be someone.
I want to be more than someone.
I want to have something to show for this life.
I want to push my way up.
I want to force my way to greatness.
In this dark spackle of night, I know there is kindness.

2

At the gym, the other day, an elderly woman asked me for help.
She was at the top of the stairs coming down, and I was walking
up, sweaty, purpled and exhausted. She asked, 'Will you do me
a favor?' I said, 'Sure.' She said, 'Will you carry this bag down
to the bottom of the stairs for me?' I said, 'Yes.' I think about
the things we do for one another and the things we don't do; the
things we will continue to do despite uneasiness, despite fear,
despite cruelty, and change. I shudder at what might rise to my
lips, about what mountains might separate us from one another,
and what mountains might separate us from ourselves.
There must be kindness despite the possible end of the world.

3
the dead wooden stars of my tongue
the dead wooden rolling of thunder

will nothing come to bless what has a chance to spring?
will nothing stand for what once was ruined?

love to slaughter it all
love to bring it all down   bloodied

TRANSLATION

Abruptly, something spruced in me.
In the blood of my fist, in the blood
Of my eye. Something whispered
Inside, *don't be afraid*. It was
A small day. It was a small way
To see the dust storm within. To see
The way I inhaled the odor of what
Bred inside. There is what you
Do and what you don't do. There is
The heart you are given and the
Heart you follow. Mine is great
And big and full. What else is there
To follow? The breaking was first.
The wild shoot stalking up within
Me. The squeaky wrung of my
Breath. I didn't feel the desire then.
I couldn't translate my fear into
Action, so it tumbled out of me.
Fate taunted with a metal-tipped
Tongue. I learned. I am ensnared in
My own history. I am one woman in
This awful world. I look at all the
Wooded fears of me, the lowland
Suns of me, and my dark-sparked
Dreams. All the nimble scraps of
Hope I feed myself. I stop. I listen.
We live many lives, a friend tells
Me. I stop being afraid. I need to
Bring something fixed and fragrant
Into this uncertainty. I need to flame
Back the tatters of dreams past. I
Need to prove to myself that I can
Live the life I want, despite

Darkness, despite doubt, despite
Fear, and despite my sex. I am so
Tired of wondering *when* and *how*.
I am so tired of limping through this
World alone. I will build my life
With song and language. I am
Doing it now with hope and dreams,
Blessings and reprieves. All the
Good ways I hold myself captive to
Myself. They will outweigh what is
Struck-down and riddled in ash. The
Phoenix relights its own fire. I am
Lighting my spark with heart.

WRUNG

It is not the heart twisting and turning. It is not the talking back of the heart, for the heart knows how to whittle experience, how to feel something akin to a spine. Yes, it is about becoming. *Wrung*. It is not a spiky thing and it has no tentacles, though it is feeling. That mechanism of defense can bring about glory, can bring about the moment where a girl becomes. *Wrung*. Sticking words together, the heart beats sound and in that sound is snot, blood, and tears. There is much more here that is animal, not human, not star-light, not sea-rasp. *Wrung, wrung, wrung* again. This is not a platonic love story between two lovers, but a love story between the heart and the self. *Wrung*. I will throb you. I will shelter you; I will shatter you. We can swing this. We can take this. We can gut it and line it. Red is a color of blood and the color of birth and the color of faith. *Wrung*. Let's take the writer out of the experience. All these words are nested in heart. *I am your only love,* it says. *I am your only life,* it says. *I am your only, only.* Love me.

WHEN LIVING FEELS LIKE A LABOR OF LOVE

It begins the way it always does,
whether it's a movie, a song,
or some snippet overheard on the subway.
There is heartbreak.
On the television:: heartbreak.
On the internet:: heartbreak.
Meeting a friend for drinks:: heartbreak.

What is wrong with us?

I keep trying to make sense of the rules:
goodness, patience, respect, and freedom.
Maybe these things need to be spoken out loud.
These silent struggles need to be lined up and fought for.
They need some kind of upheaval.
We are the ones to blame.
We do not love enough.

This is not a phenomenon.

The heartbreak is the passed-over sign
that no one reads and no one wipes clean
because we are numb to the grime and to the wear.
We know better, but the heartbreak;
The heartbreak is everywhere.

News travels so fast on Twitter,
but it's just too much for the heart.
I know no decade is better,
madness is madness,
and every age has its chaos.

A REAL POEM

1

In love, there are times where unprecedented things happen.
I'll just say it here: I have never been to battle,
but I battle every day.

We speak a part. Studies show this. We speak a part,
as we are made of parts. We are partly made of mothers.

2

There's only two moments in a life, but I don't want to talk about
authority. I know there is no expiration date.

3

The great bird of me is on guard.
The great bird of me is discovering the floor and the ceiling of this life.
I am not endorsing dramatics; I am merely stating the obvious.
Everything comes down to power.

4

I'm not interested in conquest, but in value.
We can decide the way we are spoken to.
I am deciding it now.

5

I can hear hope everywhere.
Poetry is lonely times,
but poetry is also language,
and also, social.
It is about personhood.
I choose sound.
It is a way to enter.
It is a way.

2
PEOPLE WANT
THEIR LEGENDS

ALL MY DAYS AT THE OPEN DARK

stand in an always
so often as I am, as I be, as I will
above the grit of good and arriving

                    any ways
dark has no face and dark runs from the moon

but wolves in the teeth of night,
                    the clank and the gong

                    sit, here
hover   utter   still
a sourcing   a re-affirming
        a waited rush of the found
        a vein like a star's violet
or blue
            or navy, in vain

SECONDHAND

The telling of this tale is secondhand and thick.
I quarrel with myself to believe.

There is little time, and I hand
myself seconds of happy recordings.

Who loves the way I dream myself into spirit,
the way I second-guess,

or the way I defend all my glories?
I know this is nothing but secondhand

nonsense. In this land of mistake,
my heart becomes an offering of second-helpings.

I don't remember falling second to myself,
neglecting the long table of my heart.

How did I do this to myself?
I have become secondary.

I WANT TO BE STARK [LIKE]

A man is only worth what people say he is,
and those Starks are good stock. They'll knee-deep it.
They famish the craving they are fathered by.
Manning the forestry of life, they are steadfast and sturdy.

When pungent or cruel, they sauce the ache.
Light folds them in two.
What I want to say is, *I would meet you upon this.*

Let me, too, carry the token of the world.
Tell me the secret of what comes next,
and then take me

river   river   river

KHALEESI SAYS

In this story, she is fire-born,
knee-deep in the shuddering world.

In this story, she knows no fear,
for what is fractured is a near-bitten star,
a false-bearing tree,
or a dishonest wind

In this story, fear is a house gone dry.
Fear is *not* being a woman.

I am no ordinary woman, she says,
My dreams come true.

and she says and she is
and I say, *yes, give me that.*

TYRION SAYS

I wish I was the monster you thought I was,
Tyrion says,
      and I think, *how we all return to our places.*
You can see the gods clutch as he waits for a low sky,
for a corner of hope.
      I've been on trial my whole life, he says
and nails the iron tip on the tooth.

A sleeping evil, though dumb on night, is still an evil,
but Tyrion is no heathen, though he is slight.

He says, *I wish I had killed him,*
but even the dark has its blossoms,
and his are green-tipped and tart.

This is the law of the land, my friend,
of fathers,
of men,
of words.

The saw cuts right through an ugly thing
blood is ugly but pure
blood clots
blood congeals
blood reveals
      [doesn't it?]

I saved you all from a monster, he says,
[and he did, but that's another matter]

Tyrion is another kind of monster,
a kinder monster.

This one is sore-footed;
this one is lion-hearted;
this one is high-watered in good.

I want to say, *this will soon be a time long ago,*
so, play on,
dwarf,
liege,
Lannister.

KHALEESI SAYS (REPRISE)

I will fight injustice with justice, she says,
and *I bring you a choice.*
But what if she said, *you will obey me.*

That pride is a pit,
and Khaleesi is no peach.
Brute. Burden. Beast.
She is bullied, brazen and bare.

She has scrabbled with man, horse and spirit.
What is fire-born can be fire-ridden,
for one hand has five fingers.
One digit could lead the others astray.

This hand is reaching up
as she is of the air.

She says, *I will see each of their faces.*
When she says *each*, she means, *all.*
What if, in the moment that she leans in close
to the lens, there is a smear of sap?
What then of womanhood?

A Mother of Dragons
is still a mother.

Her stare is blue:
a fire not catching.
A stunted sun.
A contorted kiss.
A vein left-turned.

This hand gives allegiance,
and this hand, the heart.
And her heart beats

with the roar of a wingspan
so big it could cover us all
in darkness.

CERSEI

She walks for all of us. A lead-and-follow dance. Arrow-backed, and hell-fired. A drawn gun, a broken suffering and a horned-spur.

She is an emblem of ache. A hanging fire, pale but burning. Pale but smoking still. Pale and stuttering with spark. Her walk is a public machine, a gear of submission, of repulsion, and the subversion of seeing. She is a heroine of hate. A thick-bloodied sinner. Warrior. Woman.

This is for all the women who love too much
shame
for all the women who love too little
shame
for all the women who have said, No
shame
for all the women who have given too much
shame
for all the women who have happily taken
shame
for all the women who know their worth
shame
for all the women who have reason
shame
for all the women who have given in
shame
for all the women who do not apologize
shame
for all the women who try
shame

for all the women who believe
shame
for all the women who despair
shame
for all the women who are not helpless
shame
for all the women who save themselves
shame
for all the women who know what they want
shame
for all the women who know their worth
shame
for all the women who will not compromise
shame
for all the women who say it isn't enough
shame

IN MY NEXT LIFE, I WANT TO BE AN AD MAN

I want to be donned in *somehow*. Donned in *everything*. Donned in the forgotten and the ecclesiastics of sex. Drape me in the charged. Drape me in the raptured. Drape me in meaning and keep it private. I want two lives: one in the city and one in the country. Two women: a blonde and a redhead. Drape me in wealth. Drape me in booze. Don me in diamonds and fur. Drape a secretary, here, and then, there.

[*Executive* is the word that comes to the lips and they smile for you, sister.]

Don me in designer suits. Don me in a new age. Don me in what's coming. Drape the future round my shoulders. Drape the next life across my lap. Drape me in the madness. Don me in the twoness of passion. Don me in pieces of last, of force; pieces of shaken and possible then drape me in manhood. Drape me in machinery and steel. Don me in utterly and *plush utterings* and, [do I sound like I'm stuttering?] make me look good; the world is dangerous.

THE TIMES

When Don puts on the *Revolver LP* it is like I'm back in my childhood bedroom asserting that it is not the 1990s. When the Beatles terrorize his penthouse apartment, I wish I could sit on his lap and sing to him.

Don says, 'Having a dream is admirable.'

He can drink all he wants, as long as when 'And Your Bird Can Sing' comes on he promises to dance. Whiskey could do the trick. Those Drapers are pretty predictable. Drapers do whatever they want. Even if Don is an 'ideas man', he knows better than to say 'No' to a woman.

Don says, 'Raised in the 30s, my dream was indoor plumbing.'

Megan says, 'Don, *you're* everything I dreamed.'

Let's not talk about my dreams…

I thought I'd hate Don, like everyone else, but I don't. I long for him the way kids long for the turning of the Ice Cream Man. I hear that elevator door DING and I rise on up.

Sure, he's troubled like the rest of them, but beneath that designer suit is a good, strong man. He's a warrior. He treats Joan like she came out of that goddamn Trojan horse with the soldiers, all woman, all beauty and all power-hungry as hell. She's everything a man is and more. Don can't plead with Joan; she's a woman who's ready to kill her darlings.

I know advertising is based on moments, but so is life. Don has changed this moment for me.

When Don falls asleep on Peggy's lap, you can feel the continents shift. He almost tells her she's beautiful, but doesn't, which is good, because she doesn't need that from him. When her number's called, she gets gone.

When she gives her notice, he takes her hand like she is royalty. He is tender and sensual. It is almost erotic in the way he lingers there in the twilight of her moment. She is rejecting him and he won't let go of her hand. She feels his lips, not on her face, but on the top of her hand; her fingers; and her nails.

He is proud of her; she's her own glory now. She's got the guns and the ammo, but inside, I bet he's thinking:

I've created a monster.

Peggy resists all the clichés and wraps herself in strength. She takes Don on in the way that children learn to fight back tears.

This is tough-love at its finest.

It's a man's world, but not for all of us.

MY WAY

Don has authority and Peggy has the emotion, but that's in the past.
She wears the pants, Don cries alone in his apartment, and Peggy lives in the not-knowing
Each breath a gasp.
Don lives 'in the now' and 'the know', but what *does* he know?
His failures are a ladder she climbs rung by rung.
Together, they are two parts of a stumbling whole. Their past, a sawed-up truth.
One small tear at an ankle, could bring them to their knees.

When Peggy needs Don, he is glad to be needed. It is that need that creates desire.
That needing is a haunt.

Peggy asks, 'What do I know about motherhood?' and Don takes a moment.
He simmers in their intellects and lets her burn.
She looks at him, and says, 'You love this,' and she's right, he does, but not in *that* way.
He loves her for what she is capable of. She is Manhattan, a metropolis.
Her arms pulse with the blood of this century and the next.

Their warring turns to music, and they dance to Sinatra. It is as sweet as every childhood memory they wish they had, except she is not a child and he is not her father.

There is a tenderness there, in their package of equals.

Their sale is not dependent on their cleverness.
Their sale is not dependent on their skill.
Their sale is dependent on their love for one another,
and on their love in one another.

Peggy puts her head on Don's shoulder,
and the moon is a face of want.
Their love is pinned in the stars of the city.
Their love is based on this want.
For they both only know one way, *my way*.

DON DREAMS AND I DREAM

So, Don dreamt he was an angel. It's sweet. I've dreamt about motherhood. [So what?] Now, it feels downtrodden. I wish I knew the crested. I wish I knew what made the light twitch; what brings the light to the moon so I can carry it inside, and know there is glory in the in-between. That there is something here to be sought or sought-after. Something to be stared-down beautiful.

> *I dreamt I was an angel. When a man walks into a room, he brings his whole life with him. I bring golden cornhusks, green apples and dung.*

I want to dream an idea that is birthed through a carnival's sawdust floor. I want to dream you and let you ride into the night – all shaky-hinges and crated-screams. I want you to ferris to me. Oblige to gravity. I want your fall to be planned.

★

[Do you even want that kind of attention?]

[I want the aftermath. That germinating.]

[I won't let go of this.]

[I won't let you.]

PEOPLE WANT THEIR LEGENDS

In the would-be version, a hero, or patriot is needed.
We'd have nothing but our own hearts to listen to.

There is a fear of contradiction.
As the story goes, the hero provides what they see fit.

I want to be that.
I want a shifting of place in your chest.

The real danger is sport
and the most romanticized sport is love.

I want something to rally about.

The believing is pure-like: *you do,*
                              you don't, you do,

you don't, you do, you don't.

You have the final whistle.

The final call.
The final sip.

Pull yourself together.
This is more powerful than myth.

HEART

The worst thing you can do to these people is be yourself.
– Azar Nafisi, from a reading at Hunter College, February 21st 2017.

In the shared space of our mercy, remember
the age of fantasy. Forget
the idea of coming out of something, a past or future. Clasp
the decision, the indecision, that struggle, and move on.
Anything important, any thing, any pursuit is worth it. Anything
generous and wondrous is a river of good, and without problem.
The many-chambered lack of curiosity is flammable,
unshakable and bigger than you, or I. Or,
it has to do with how you do what you do, when there is so much to do. Leave
the fear behind; you don't know where life takes you. It's the way the pounding
of days dreams you forward, far-flung and believing. Trust
it; it is like falling in love again. It is a ladder
to hope. I tell myself *go after the heart*. And I do, and I won't apologize.
This self is all I've got: my heart, this life, the heart, it.

3
A HISTORY OF
SWORN WAYS

CARNAGE

Everyone is saying *no* to me.
Just as they do now,
Just as they will.
It is a kind of civil riot,
A staged parade.
It makes every kind of sense.
That carnage that comes with falling hard.
That carnage that hassles and times.
That carnage that language picks up.
I am wanting to be picked up,
And it is rarely an accident.
Elements are employed.
Pounds are ranged.
The number of possible routes are lost,
All to force my foot door to door,
To match the heart of my drive to
Coffee after coffee after coffee.
Take me as a whole.
Take these birds outside my window,
Alive with the everyday thrill of
Worm or bug or crumb. Take them,
Then remember my thrills.
Everyone is saying *no* to me,
And I am flummoxed each time
I ask for more; or try for more.
I strive, and I strive.
That's the 21ˢᵗ century calling.
It's doable. I travel great lengths,
So, I can match my heart
With the focus of each and every obstacle.
Can there be a rallying point?

This is not an accident.

(Is that what I should be learning here?)

Well, isn't that magnificent.

CONTEMPORARY HISTORY

I

At the Emily Dickinson exhibit at The Morgan, I look at Emily's digital book of pressed flowers. I am impressed at her range, at her care, and her attention.

All her parts are intact: leaves, stigmas and stamens.

It is a beautiful thing, her art, and her flaunting of nature, but those specimens are trapped.

My friend says, goes to show you how much time women had on their hands back then, and I laugh, but it isn't funny. Even I know time is both pleasure and curse.

2

What more could Emily have done? What more could have been of her life? How have I kept my life intact? What about my pressings?

3

Later, at dinner, I fill my friend in about my dating life. I layer my delight with pepperings of despair. My dangers in waiting. My distaste for games. My unwillingness to follow time and enjoy the present. I say it is hard for me; because it is hard for me. I can't pretend otherwise. These are my crosshairs and my skippings. My overflooding cannot be dammed. And what of my indulgent worrying that I can't disturb or shove off?

I talk about expectations. What I want, favor and rely on. I think about what my sister says about my going from 0 to 10. How I'm so ready to fall in love, I'm already there.

How can that be wrong?

My friend says, expectations are good. She says, it boils down to the mothers. They raise their sons to be princes when they should really be raising them to be kings.

NOTES TO THE MOTHERBOARD

Mother, this is slow-loading. Why don't we just go plant our own
pods? Plug into the wild of the wired. No need to add a voice to
this whirring. This cloud of analog and dialogue and *Once Upon a
Dial-Up.*

      I'll be the first to say it, *a good domain name is hard to find.*
(Especially if you're jonesing for the perfect one).

                                 The pickings are slim.
A Cliff, Dick or Harry could get caught in the spam. I'll keep to it.
Keep needling the hay,
and the time between reloads, refreshes, rescans.

[Auto-remind: maybe Norton can help de-script this technobabble
baloney?]

What happened to clean? To pure? To loyal? We're just caught in
the filth and the cached,
the auto-fill and the default.
                          Predict what's coming.
Translate the page into French. Change my background to pretty-
like. Pretty is as pretty does. You big pretty-brained tinker toy.
You can't even talk back.

                          [How do you like them apples?]

FOR THE BLONDES

know, that all is yellow
      as in a day

that day and this day
the sweet drums in growth
and the short shift of light is done

none know that I would've lifted this,
and you, skybound

                    I would've swung your swing and clampt it hard

I am not a heavyweight
but I know a moment

this is not despair, but a forgetful storm
where I was rapt, and you were rapt
all in a grinning gag

                (it was good)

only half of my mumble is mumble
and the other half is blonde
but the calm
belongs to its ends

take my hand and hold its end
in it is decades of excited songs.
those, I would sing.

      (those I do sing)
here,
      listen.

HOLDING

I am the one holding the wheel
             & the one tying us to the mast.

Mated.
        Unmated.

               I am handling the tugs and pulls.

The night golds black; it gullies calm in the spins of sea-light.
I tremble at the undertow.
The sea sounds of stresses.

               I handle the stresses.
The fallacy is breathing.

The questions fade with salt.

                                                    Use the lack.

The moist is for the heavy hearted.

We are light.

We throw the rocks not yet cast.

          Count with me: *one*   *two*   *three.*

I have questions.

They turn their bellies up at me.

                              Naked.
                              No shame.

            I do not judge.

I have no opinions.

I bare my throat,

a laugh.

The tides are timed.

I can almost see you.

The sea scallops the truth, parting the stink.

What is important is the cutting of the tide.

The slicing of foam.

The nightwalk of the moon.

The way we sleepwalk together.

I bend my shoulders for you.
I bare the translucent.
          You are not yet aboard.

I am warming the seas.

the sea inside is not random

to await the whaled fate

to go before the unhoused

this piece
                              this bone
          this knot

master the settling

                                        the charred
          the ached

gather the un-netted
                    wave the hope drift afar

see the heart water blue

see the dusk bleed black

gather the dark

now, hold.

IN SEVENTEENTHS

I'm a natural networker; I provide an alternative
when I want. I'm a natural ponderer.
I just know some things; the way ants know
their way home. Knowing my psychology, I know
how to raster my thirst for glory; for what is tender;
for what buttons me to truth. I occupy what is round,
what is housed inside this body.

> *Nothing is perfectly nailed to the walls.*

I have stolen the revolutionary experience from the past;
I have been strange and savage.

                              I know the heart,
and how it goes on beyond the Social.

> *Life's rich pageant.*

I crave the savory and the sweet. I feel certain
that it will all happen soon. I will keep the singing
loud inside me. I will keep this song that makes all
other songs feel *verklempt*.

THE LITTLE WAR

The heart cannot speak. The stomach cannot see. The kidney cannot
hear. The liver cannot taste. The eyes cannot feel. They lack.

In this little war, the speed of the eye is *null* and akin to nothing.
No one knows this.

Together, we do not move or forage or forest. *Reader,* what do you
know of muteness?
Of the world so strange and of the haunt of numbers?

I want

to know what you carry

…there…

(If it is a key,   *give it*.)

It feels like a battle. A hidden one. A hidden, little, one. Subtle-like,
where my feet do not leave prints. The air does not capture my breath.
My hair does not hit the floor; it flies up to a tree where it harvests a
nest for someone/thing else. Nothing shoots. Nothing loads. No thing
screams, but I know something inside *wants.*

I don't know what is beneath the exterior, or the virtual. I am losing.
Alignment is losing. Thought is losing. Feeling is latching to some
thing, some where.

What happened to the story?

when?

                                        What happened to the tale?

how?

                        Say that someone, somewhere knows.

reach

                Reach me.

LONELY IS A HARD WORD TO USE IN A POEM

I'm resisting the trained crows. I know the routine.
I know the cue and the call and the old shuffle-ball-chain.

I want you to say, *stop, let me take this one on*.

SOS

Don't make light of my personal experiences
for I am also red-wheeled and screaming.
Each of us must make do in the best way we can.
Love and duty are not always aligned.
But for me, they are a steady rung I climb.

Here's some extra.
After the witty responses,
the sharp bites,
the meanings are suffused with burden
and gilded in urgency.
The insular ferocity reminds us that
we have rituals, trials and triumphs.
Here, I can speak as myself
and with a certain authority.
A certain collective.

Listen.

//

There is a light in me.
Unavoidable, mistrusted.
There is a light in me
that surges in the dark
corners of each day.
There is a light in me.
It comes up.
It goes out.

It comes up.
It goes out.
It's a sort of story
I write in staccato.
Sometimes a farce.
Sometimes high drama.
This twinkling
is a call to others.
A distress warning
do you see?

THE REST

Go on, the thriving lifts,

    the thriving and the shift, the thriving delivers the quips.

       Yes, it is difficult to say what to do; *Yes,* it is
       difficult to say what to say; *Yes,* it is difficult.
       Yes, it is difficult. I know it is difficult. It is
       all so very difficult but many live to know.

Time is as helpless as an uneaten breakfast.
I will wait – eggshells and all.
The rest ought to be good.
               ★

When I came to the top, I saw the later moon. At the top, I saw the
later stars, too, and one came down to me, a real roadmaker, and
said, *I know you,* and then in the laterdust, I saw the pulling back of
night, and then, there were motions.
There were howled longings. There were nests still warm to the
touch. I *felt* they were still warm to the touch.

                I know; I know; I know, I am alone
and this thing is late and feather-laden. I am still moved, though it
is difficult to say

                             how

Don't they know?
    Don't they know, I cherish the bristle and the fat?

BLOOM

I wouldn't want to define myself in a single sentence. So much is already orchestrated.

★

Sometimes, I hate that   every   little   thing   comes down to 'love' for me.

A friend tells me that she hopes that I'm happy. Another, that she is disappointed in most people. Another, that she feels dead inside. Heartless.

★

I walk a lot, but I'm usually quite serious. I smile at dogs. I smile at children. Sometimes I treat the sky to a flash, but in the waiting room of my heart, there is a long line circling. Too much is held down by weights.

I saw a little boy the other day with his mother. He smiled up at her screaming with delight, 'I'm so happy!' His mother responded, 'I'm glad you're happy.'

It was a quick moment but a consolation. I still think of the fearlessness he possessed in saying just how he felt. That innocence. That good despite the world. Sometimes, that's all it takes, either a brush of honesty or a flipping off. Sometimes, you have to just acknowledge it, say *fuck it*, I'm happy today, *fuck it*, I'm miserable, or *fuck it*, this is out of my control. That sort of self-telling is a technique away from torture, a dive away from sadness. It is the bait to haul me out of the murk and up and over to stretches of fortune. It isn't easy to be positive and strong. I'm tired of that directive dominating me. I'm tired of holding myself up.

★

On Instagram today, I saw that it was Lady Gaga's birthday. She posted how she needs to remember to be grateful more, and to be more reflective. These are darkly-framed days. It is an easy thing to be grateful, but not so easy to recognize the way that relief is implemented. I could be more generous with myself, too. There is a relief in knowing I am who I am, and a relief in knowing that each day I try to be my best self, but each day is a heed to a trick or a tangent.

★

My sister says, maybe everything is leading you to this moment and there's the optimism in a single phone call. That's the latch I'll swing on. That knowing of how a moment can bloom.

HERE IS MY OFFERING

I have given it 110% every day. I flout the reckless.
Each time I undo the bare, I bury the slights. It is a kind of slaughter.
I cannot see what other women do or don't do.
In true time, empty still equals empty, but I consent.
I hear the bell ringing. I am aware of the crests and the falls:
Those are the day rustlers and I am unafraid.
I want an index to polka through. I could choose: *B* or *G* or *L*
And see where the throes swell. I believe I can throw it.
One day, there will be a rushing, and one day, I will lurch forward,
Sing through the cabin of me,
And pin down the madness of this world one tack at a time.
And, this sloping bite, this blood-drawn tease, this wide-combed life,
I will let it all run loose. I will excite dreams with color.
I will be trusting, even-shuffled and thirsty.
Don't let me lose my way.
There is a thrumming I can still hear.

FOLLOW

Follow where all is / follow the transfused/ follow what is still and what is still-attracting.
That light / that beauty / that love / that, that is massy-borne and rising-up, like a drifting star.

Like stars lift / Like lifting stars./ Like the lifting of stars, I rose. I rise.

Rose. Rose. Like a thing beyond words: satiated.

Let lie in the ravage / Let lie in what is ravaged-wrought

Why fear what hasn't become?

I beckon, like light. / Like a star, I will beckon. / You will oblige. / You will lend the want.

You will eclipse my blinding. You will know nothing. Nothing. You will know nothing of what has been dark.

A SCENE FROM A PROPER SPITE

There are back alleys of candor and private rendering of words.
In my opening is a shattering howl. I am overbred, and overbaked
with a gut that is funded by fritters. Do you know the murdering lusts,
the secret deposits of night keepings and black dressings?

We are always banking.

I am tired of the way I am always running, of the way I lower my legs
and no spur falls. I am tired of being horizon-bound.

I've read the stories and each of your confidences.

I've made corrections.

What is truffled in turmoil is unspoken.

I raise my shield again.

I step closer to the understanding. There are so many ways to commit.
There are so many ways to be committed. I will commit this to memory.
I defend myself in the unstinting kiss of comfort.

This is not seductive.

This is an inflammation, a festering, an epidemic of the heart.

THIS IS TO CALM YOU WHEN YOU ARRIVE

The world is open, is opening up, but know that in any unannounced
moment, we could steam a real diversion. The storm, that vulnerability, is as tall
as a five-star province, as the largest vortex of my lungs, or the plushest chair

of my heart. Remember, I am building this from the ground up. I am merely a person
on the fence between wanting and just getting it myself. I walk this sidewalk
narrating my pioneer ways and there is so much disgrace that ascends
from the swoon of heat in my breath, to the whole damn building of my body.

Every day, I use this broadness, this key to quarantine the hurt,
to shepherd this all away from me: desire, thirst, revulsion. I am the only one knocking.
I was told I am good enough. I was told to believe *you* are good enough.
Open this stumbling. Open this button-breaking day, and tear the page of my tongue.

Accept the clumsy end of being human. Take the shabby out.
Take my garbled story out, and tell me not to fear my own goodness.
Finger the fury, the girlish universe at my feet, the fastening secrets full of lost causes
and clauses, for I know the floating empire inside me. Soon, a gale will come
to blow away the spurn, to blow away this horrible machine, and the guilt. *Oh, the guilt.*

SOMETIMES THE ANGELS ARE DEVILS
Inspired by W.B. Yeats' 'The Second Coming'

Sometimes the angels are devils and we are all in a gyre,
but of course, there are alternate ways of looking. The falconer
is just a man, and men are shutting themselves off. They can't hold
on to interests or feelings. Boredom is a new four-letter word,
and so is pride. *All men must die,* is a mock battle-cry, but fires are everywhere.
Mine are real, not self-made, but man-made, and they will not be drowned.
I am the subject of my own life, a friend, an enemy at times, but my worst
face is softer than most. These are troubling times with such hallowed intensity
                                    and spiked-musting.

There are daily messengers at hand,
they open my heart, they feed from my hand,
and sometimes, the imagination shuts, whispering *outoutout,*
but let's get back to the minute particulars of life and spirit.
I will lift away the despair with a flick of my wrist, and I will desert
the false hopes, those torn pages, and the wolfed-heart I've manned
with a force so bright, truth looks away. Moons, stars, suns
look away. You see, there are a handful of stories inside us. They, we, it
know what our sacrifice means. They live in our boxing, as a bird
in her nest. You need this to align, and I want something untypical;
something that doesn't want to lay alone, stir alone, sleep alone,
alone, something that isn't afraid of a tender-failure, or a cradled-mystery.
Last night, I was a star. I was in orbit and the whirl of night was glorious. Last
night, I picked up my own force, to keep the good going; and the sad,
                         pushed off, into the past, and back-borne.

THE HALLUCINATION

I work at the hallucination,
and the clang of me is an intimate shuffle.
I sometimes work myself into a blinding snub,
nudging, at the threat that will never be over.
I wasn't legislating. Sometimes, I am barely legible,
but it is incomprehensible to say that I have never arrived.

★

I arrived after the freezing-out:
the collarbone, after-exposed
the lean neck. It was all to faun my motor.
To blaze it all.
Let me rebroadcast it, for I see it everywhere.
I won't say *vixen,* but blockbuster.
I like that.

★

Remember, yes remember,
I've halved the nights in two.
And at some polarity, or poky, I resisted collapse.
The bee, the cat, the blue jay,
the nightingale, the wolf, the horse,
the woman, *yes, the woman,*
we all have the same thirst.

STRANGER IS: AN AMERICAN LIFE

That it might have been yesterday,
But here we are, and it is astonishing.
The hidden and the rejected fall off.
The chaotic firsts, the exiled words, the discovery
                                        of lie upon lie.
Don't let them.
            Don't let them forget to say their name aloud.
Remember, this volume of our future is overwhelmed
By what is vivid. This sensory overload is fashioned in the air,
Thick with blossom and ripe with insult.

                                  Exhale.
There is so much in this to adore:
The coming together   the discussion,
The ardent resistance,   and the next generation,

conspiring   re-evaluating   flowering

Don't forget the horror. The unrelenting slog,
The brain-noise   the steeping-must of hate,
The mulling-over of falsehoods.
It is too much to keep to one's self.

I have hopes here, still unquelled.
Within our bodies, inside,
Is another inside,
            And another inside,
                   And another inside that,
                         Like a procession of thrones.

Peel back the gilded.
Be kind to yourself, but notice the shifting of hands.
Think about how things are casted,
        The tangible things.
Those that used to be casted by hands,
Are now spun in lies.

                    ★

I am disappointed in my country's dreams,
In my countless dreams, and in my country of dreams.
I am most disappointed in my own inability to see.
I keep saying to myself, darkness doesn't hold, and it won't,
                                So, don't close.

Think: beacon, reckon rage,
And then fathom the unthinkable.
                        This is not a country that stops.

TRUTH

I make
little markings.
Each letter
of every word,
a foot alive.

//

Abandoning is a rock.
Abandoning is a rock lodged
in a throat so tight,
it can hardly compromise
the lonely air.
This rock has its comfort.
It builds a house within its chest
& the abandoning closes its eyes
seeing what it remembers:
that life is good.

//

A year.
What changes
in a year?

Age?
Nails?
Skin?
The body?

People?
No.

A year is
a gathering.

SONNET

I cannot horse the dark concerns

That move into the timeless day. Say

It is easy to learn the lovelorn ways, to learn

The freckled longing, the phantom urge for what is not yet stone.

Disobey. Disobey. I try to disobey my looking for stops. Here, I will tell you

My conclusion. Here, in the noon shade, in this migrating truth, I wish for what is pure,

For what is not a loud confusion of wrong. For the way the world spins,

A design of sweeps and steps and turns.

All the sobering voices of my despair and all of these, well, these too-felt days.

We are mere creatures: we tower, we crawl, we cower, we saw.

We saw the way it could go. We pocket the touchless, the heartless, and more.

We corridor the periods of near-survival. We reform the weeds, seal the dark shade

Of monsters made, and marvel. We marvel at what is good. (Sometimes we need a good stare.)

We hope for love and bask in the harrowed flux of tomorrow: its vision, sound and green.

WHEN BOYS BECOME WEREWOLVES

When boys become werewolves
they come back stronger
to suffer

after the very soft life
feats relate to feats

say, *next*
say, *more*
say, more to me next week
and falsify the known

Even the readiest marks
can run. Harvest, here. And tell me, *how*
and let the lunar lie. Rustle here. Lie to me.

One moon. Four stars. Two girls. One car. One wish. One moon.
Four Stars. Two girls. One car. One wish. One moon. Four stars.
Two girls. One car. One wish. One moon. Four stars.

POEM IN WHICH I ADDRESS MYSELF

You aren't being robbed of time,
   you're just trying to get out of your landmarks.
You're being robbed of the present by thinking of the future.
You know that, Leah. Let me lead you behind the curtain.
Here, are the levers, the smoke-screens, the horns.
Here, are the buttons, the knobs and the toggles.
Let's turn to something new: nonsense.
Everyone has their offences, Leah, yours, well,
I laugh to think of what yours are, but it is probably
the heart you wear on your sleeve and your unnerving need for love.
We are an empire that hasn't fallen. We are an empire
that hasn't fallen yet, but all good things must end,
mustn't they? I know what you'll say, *they don't have to,*
and you're right. Let's ride that wave. Every story you've
ever read is a golden treat. I will tell you a new one, now.
We are an endless line that will ultimately break
or never break, or break several times before
re-generating like a starfish. Ah, that beauty.
Think of the organisms. One small step for mankind.
One small sludge up shore. The braid of such sea-songs.
There is a *why* to these things. There is such a thing
as a 'good fail', and *you* know better than most.
Determining what your *sometimes* is, is always the hardest part.
Let's see where the kick is here. Writing is creating.
This poem is a creation. Is it monumental? (no)
Will it change the world? (unlikely)
Can it be a backdrop for a natural process where the world
keeps gurgling, keeps destroying and rebuilding,
burning and cooling? (yes) All things yearn, Leah.
Desire is natural. Keep the story alive.
All tales hinge from another tale.

Yours starts with words.
We all send messages.
All you have to do is look.

SELF-PORTRAIT

You are welcome for all the times I have not said *no*. You are welcome for letting you know I am not perfect. You are welcome for letting you know this struggle. You are welcome for the ways that I have opened this up without fear of the scalpel of this world. You are welcome for the way I navigate the world's difficult ways without love; you are welcome for my fearless beauty.

And what of my desperate letting-go of hope and all of my strong-willed lacklusters, those darker frustrations? You are welcome. And you, you are welcome for all my overachieving that *suggests* loss. You are welcome for my history of feelings.

Thank you for this heart. Thank you for the woman that I am.

SURVIVAL

My whole life I've been the speaker of my poems, but that isn't really true. My voice came late, sympathetic, like a witness, or a victim. It was a rescuing impulse: that art. We were already groping at each other through the flower-sprayed fields of self-discovery. All across this body, I felt I was winning. I felt the harshness of promise conspire with the transformation of story, my story. We all have stories, like the way all states have fear.

This is a feared state but we must open the doors of our hearts, and let the latches fall. All futures are uncertain. A brave new world is one where doom and sight are equivocal. Look again, this isn't fiction; we are living this.

At times, the extraordinary overtakes me. A kiss, a new book, a moment of flattery, laughter or a happy mistake. The dream, the scene of the past, and the present are all encounters like train travel. The moment passes through us before we register the scene, but I want to register this.

I want to remember my hope and my heart. I want to remember the way time skips forward and away, like the stunning sight of bird-wings beating, that stirred fascination, that flutter and art. Yes, I said *art*, and it is, even in this pacing of life we propel ourselves through.

The wild joy is in the speaking. We must keep speaking. We are all in some way depressed, and the undepressed is in the imagining of desertion. The imagining of the next moment, the next day, the next year, like a rift opening. Keep looking. Manipulate that violating. Manipulate the whirl of your anger and meld it to what stirs you.

In T. H. White's *The Once and Future King,* Merlin tells the young King Arthur, The Wart, that he will someday face all the evil in the world. He says, 'Learning will never fail you,' and I feel that's good advice. We are all facing the darkness head-on.

Armor yourself in disruption and creation; that is the way this will end, in a forward slip into story, in taking the best parts of us into a future dawning with art and voice.

NOTES

'I Heard the Sparrows Aging' is for D. Foy
'When Boys Become Werewolves' is for Marina
'Where are the Stars' is for Sarah
'Self-Portrait; was inspired by Franz Wright's 'One Heart'
'The Rest' owes a debt to John Berryman's 'The
Lightening' and 'Fare Well'
'The Hallucination' is for Kaveh
'Translation' is for Emily
'Contemporary History' is for Heather
'Sometimes the Angels Are Devils' owes a debt to W.B
Yeats' 'The Second Coming'.
'Heart' is for Azar Nafisi, inspired by her reading and
discussion at Hunter College in 2017.

ACKNOWLEDGEMENTS

Thank you to all the editors of the journals and anthologies where the following poems have been published.
Thank you for saying *yes*.

'I Heard the Sparrows Aging', published in *Forklift, Ohio*.
'The Love-Orphans' published in *About Place Journal*.
'This Could Be Nostalgia' published in *Women's Quarterly Conversation* (online).
'For Reals', 'Hard', and 'Lonely is a Hard Word to Use in a Poem' published in *Thrush Poetry Journal*.
'Doing' published in *Jet Fuel Review*.
'When Boys Become Werewolves', published in *The Brooklyn Rail*, is for Marina Rabinovich.
'All My Days in the Open Dark' published in *Posit Journal*.
'Khaleesi Says', 'I Want to be Stark[like]' and 'Follow' published in *Poetry Magazine*.
'Cersei' and 'A Real Poem' published in *Magma Poetry* (UK).
'This Is a Love Poem' published in *The Philadelphia Review of Books* (online).
'In Seventeenths' published in *Connotation Press* (online).
'A Scene from a Proper Spite' published in *Minola Review*.
'The Little War' published in *The Mackinac* (online).
'When Living Feels like a Labor of Love' published in *Rise Up Review*.
'The Hallucination', published in *Pleiades*.
'Translation', published in *Quiet Lunch*.
'Sonnet' published in *Tinderbox Poetry Journal*.
'Stranger Is: An American Life' published in *Glass: a journal of poetry*.

'This is to Calm You When you Arrive' published in *Slice Magazine*.

'Hinge' published in *Shadowgraph Quarterly*.

'Secondhand' published in *Plume Anthology 6*.

'SOS' published in *Plume*.

'Contemporary History' published in *Barrow Street* 2018 and is for Heather Marshall.

'Carnage' published in *Queen Mob's Teahouse*.

'This is my Offering' published in *Tin House* (online) 2018.

'Turning Over Phrases: Key to Joy' – originally published in *Mercury Retrograde* anthology by Kattywompus Press (2013).

'In My Next Life I Want to be an Ad Man', 'Don Dreams and I Dream', and 'The Times' all appeared in the chapbook, *Don Dreams and I Dream* – Kattywompus Press 2014 . Editor, Sammy Greenspan.

'Forgotten Century', 'I Dreamed Up A Less Vulnerable Network', 'Where are the Stars', and 'The Love Orphans' appeared in the chapbook *Straight Away the Emptied World* – Kattywompus Press 2016. Editor, Sammy Greenspan.

Thank you to my parents, Ronnie and Arthur Umansky for being my biggest fans, and to my sister Faith Umansky for being my best friend and for always listening. I love you.

Thank you to my long-time teacher, mentor and friend, Patricia Carlin, and everyone in my beloved poetry workshop at The New School.

Thank you to Jen Fitzgerald for the beautiful author photo and for the friendship.

I am so very grateful for the friendship and support of the following friends, poets and non-poets alike (you all mean so much to me): Dena Rash Guzman, David Gutowski, Barbara Louise Ungar, Sammy Greenspan, Susan Bruce, Gina Costanza, Kelly Davio, Sarah Gerard, Tara Skurtu, Helen Vitoria, Heather Marshall, Emily-Greta Tabourin, Kaveh Akbar, Rachel Eliza Griffiths, Maggie Smith, Doireann Ni Ghriofa, Kathryn Maris, Niall Munro, Don Share, Robert Polito, Alli and Ed Brydon, Marina Rabinovich, Jill Futerman, Ellen and Drew Paulik, Tam and Louise Rodwell, Jo Young, Larry Sullivan, and of course, Graham.

I will always be thankful to everyone at Eyewear Publishing, especially Todd Swift, for giving this book a home in both the UK and the US – Truly, a dream come true! Thank you to Rosie Hildyard for all the editing, and to Edwin Smet for his creative vision.

Additional thanks to the creators, writers, actors and everyone at two of my favorite TV shows: AMC's *Mad Men* and HBO's *Game of Thrones*. You have truly changed my life with your imagination, your artistry, and your language. Thank you for the inspiration.

EYEWEAR PUBLISHING

TITLES INCLUDE